I Am Malala
Study Guide

Pembroke Notes

First published by Dog Ear Publishing
4011 Vincennes Rd
Indianapolis, IN 46268
www.dogearpublishing.net

ISBN: 978-1-4575-4069-1

This book is printed on acid-free paper.

Printed in the United States of America

INTRODUCTION

I have been teaching since 1994 with a background in elementary, special education, and secondary English. I have always been passionate about the role reading has in the learning process. In the perfect world all students would be avid readers and life-long learners. They would all blossom as individuals, cultivate knowledge, thinking and communication skills, and integrate into the real world with active voices.

I believe the English class is each student's gateway for discovering how he/she relates to language, literature, ideas, and the world. They need to read proficiently, write effectively, and critique the media that surrounds them. All materials used to master these skills should be effective and engaging while promoting critical thinking skills.

At a recent visit to the local teacher store in my hometown, I realized that 99% of the support materials supplied for the professional focused on the PreK-6 grade students. Little was available for the high school English teacher. This was when I decided to help the high school student as well as the high school teacher by sharing my study guides and notes on informational texts. This seems especially timely when states, school districts, and schools are faced with new standards that emphasize a focus on nonfiction. You will find all my materials meet the Common Core and Alaska standards.

QUESTIONS

I Am Malala

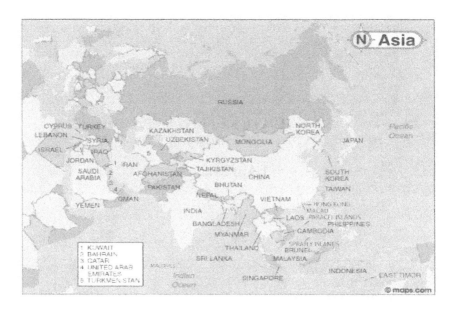

1. Locate Pakistan and all neighboring countries on this map of Asia.

2. Read the following article to familiarize yourself with the country of Pakistan.

   Pakistan Profile

3. Read the following article to familiarize yourself with the Taliban, past and present.

   The Taliban Today

PROLOGUE
Prediction

1. Malala begins her story with this statement:

    I come from a country that was created at midnight. When I almost died it was just after midday.

    What do you think Malala meant by this statement?

2. What evidence is there that where Malala is now and where her story takes place is vastly different. Where is her home now?

3. Malala and her girl friends attended school in secret. What is the evidence?

4. Behind closed doors, the mood was different. Explain.

5. What evidence showed these girls took their education seriously?

6. In some ways Malala was like any other teenager. Explain.

7. Malala excelled in school. Explain.

8. The bus was a preferred mode of transportation over walking. Why?

9. Describe the bus.

10. Describe Malala's injuries.

Part One
Before the Taliban

Rather I receive your bullet-riddled body with honor
Than news of your cowardice on the battlefield.

Traditional Pashto couplet

1.   What do you think the above couplet means?

CHAPTER 1

A Daughter is Born

Vocabulary

a. commiserated

b. auspicious

1. Culturally speaking, how are the births of girls and and boys celebrated?

2. How is Malala's father different from most Pashtun men?

3. Describe the code of Pashtunwali.

4. Our Malala is named after Malalai of Maiwand. Give a short summary of Malalai. Why is she compared to Joan of Arc?

5. Why did Malala refer to her Swat Valley as the most beautiful place in the world?

6. Summarize the history of Swat by including independence of 1947, Mad Fakir, Mingora, and Buddhism to Islam.

7. Malala valued her home in Swat. What evidence supports that fact?

8.   What purpose did a barber serve in the marriage of Malala's mother and father?

9.   Malala's father and mother do not share a traditional marriage. Explain

10. Why did Malala and her brother spend most of their time with their mother?

11. The sixteenth century proved to be devastating to the Yousafzai tribe (Malala's ancestors) in Pakistan and Afghanistan. Explain.

12. *Wesh* was a strange system of land distribution among the tribesmen. Explain.

13. Briefly describe the rule of King Miangul Abdul Wadood (Badshah Sahib) and his son Miangul Abdul Haq Jehanzeb.

14. Malala's father said of her daughter, "Malala will be free as a bird." Why did this mean so much in Pakistan?

CHAPTER 2

My father the Falcon

1. . . my father had trouble with words." Explain

2. What is the simile that describes grandfather Rohul Amin?

3. How did Lewano Pir, Saint of the Mad, try to cure Malala's father of his stutter?

4. What evidence shows that boys were valued more than girls in Pashtun families?

5. What was the impact of general Zia ul-Haq when he seized power in Pakistan? Include women's rights in court, madrasas, ISI, CIA, and Saudi Arabia.

6. Define jihad.

7. What are the five pillars of Islam?

8. How did the CIA encourage jihad?

9. Define maulana.

10. ". . .years later the same maulana's organization would become the_____."

11. How was the talib's instructions "a kind of brainwashing"?

12. What was meant by the metaphor, "war between two elephants" and the simile, "like the grass crushed by the hooves to two fierce beasts"?

13. Why might it be difficult for some Pashtuns to have a birthday party?

14. What evidence supports the fact that rivalry was significant in family dynamics?

15. Who showed Malala's father his proud path?

16. What evidence supports the frugality of Pashtuns?

17. What was Baba's (grandfather) greatest gift to Malala's father?

18. What were the results of Malala's father first speech as a boy?

CHAPTER 3
Growing Up in a School

1. Why was Malala's mother unusual in the village as a child?

2. Why was education important to Malala's father?

3. What obstacles did Ziauddin face trying to realize his dream?

4. Pakistan has a class system. Explain.

5. How did Ziauddin's fate change?

6. Why were Akbar Khan and Nasir Pacha important to Ziauddin?

7. How did Pakistan change when Benazir Bhutto became prime minister?

8. Explain The Satanic Verse by Salman Rushdie

9. Why was it important for Malala's father to start his own school?

10. Running a school is like running any other business. Explain.

11. Why did Ziauddin become a spokesman for others in education?

12. Why is a small boy brought into a marriage ceremony to sit on the laps of the bride and groom?

13. And then . . ."when it seem matters could not get worse, the area was hit by _____.

14. When did their luck change?

15. _____ would change their world, and bring war into our valley

CHAPTER 4

The Village

1. What is "woma"?

2. Describe the Eid holidays.

3. Contrast city life in Mingora and out in the Shangla valley.

4. Why does Malala question the Pashtun code of conduct?

5. How were women in Afghanistan treated?

6. "For me the valley was a sunny place and I couldn't see the clouds gathering behind the mountains" is a metaphor for what?

CHAPTER 5

Why I Don't Wear Earrings and
Pashtuns Don't Say Thank You

1. How did Malala react when the new girl, Malka-e-Noor came in first in end-of-year exams?

2. Malala was not a perfect child. Explain.

3. How did Ziauddin react to Malala's behavior?

4. Why does Malala have a problem with the Pashtunwali code?

5. Why do Pashtuns not say "thank you"?

6. Why is Malala inspired by Khan Abdul Ghaffar Khan?

7. Why were the people of Swat subservient to the new regimes?

8. How did Malala try to win back her father's respect?

9. Whom do these quotes belong: "It is far more honorable to fail than to cheat" and "teach him how to gracefully lose"?

10. What were the results of the speech competition?

CHAPTER 6

Children of the Rubbish Mountain

1. What was Malala's favorite TV show? Why?

2. Helping poor families with tuition was controversial. Why?

3. Translate: "Kia hasool e elum in bachun ka haq nahe" What is its significance?

4. How did the army feel about Ziauddin becoming a known figure in Swat?

5. What are "ghost schools"?

6. Aside from corruption and bad government, my father's main concern in those days was the _____.

7. 9/11 changed the world but how did it affect Swat?

8. How did the citizens of Swat feel about the Taliban?

9. Musharraf was double-dealing. How?

10. What measures did Malala take to help the rubbish children?

CHAPTER 7

The Mufti Who Tried to Close Our School

1. What was meant by Ziauddin's dialogue, "That maulana has a bad eye on us."?

2. What evidence supports not all Muslims think the same?

3. ". . .Muslims are split between _____ and _____. What is the implication?

5. The mufi across the street was a member of of Tablighi Jamaat, a Deobandi group. Why is this important to the story?

6. How was the controversy about the school solved?

7. How did the mufti feel about the women?

8. How was General Musharrah different from General Zia?

9. How were things different in Swat?

10. What was the Arabization of Pakistan?

11. How did MMA affect Swat?

12. What is FATA and its significance?

13. What were tribal agencies like?

14. What was the result of the army entering tribal areas in March 2004?

15. What happened June 17, 2004?

16. Why were local people shocked?

CHAPTER 8

The Autumn of the Earthquake

1. How devastating was the earthquake of October 5, 2007?

2. Where did aid come from?

3. How would you summarize the JuD and their actions after the earthquake?

PART TWO
The Valley of Death

CHAPTER 9
Radio Mullah

1. The Taliban came to the alley led by_____.

The Iron Fist of Maulana Fazlullah
www.aljazeera.com/indepth/features/2013/iron-fist-fazlullah-
2013117153826715.html

Maulana Fazlullah
timesofindia.indiatimes.com/wold/pakistan/mullah-fazlullah-
pakistan-taliban-chief-killed-in-air-strike/articlesshow/
46664643.com

2. Describe the men of the Taliban.

3. How did Fazlullah communicate with the valley?

4. How did Fazlullah appear wise to those in the valley?

5. What behaviors was Fazlullah attempting to enforce?

6. Mullahs misinterpreted the Quran and Hadith. Explain.

7. How do the militants gain support?

8. Who were the Falcon Commandos?

9. Fazlullah became more aggressive. Explain.

10. What message was taped to the school gate after the family arrived back home from Eid?

11. What is the meaning of "You have put the first stone in standing water. Now we will have the courage to speak"?

CHAPTER 10

Toffees, Tennis Balls and the Buddhas of Swat

1. When the Taliban destroyed the thousand Buddhas, they were doing more damage than smashing statues. Explain.

2. When Fazlullah came to Swat, there were no more school trips. Why?

3. How did Malala feel about the Taliban telling everyone what to do and how to dress?

4. Why did noone do anything when the Taliban attacked the police in the valley?

5. Why had the whole country gone mad?

6. What does, "When it suits the Taliban, women can be vocal and visible" mean?

7. How did the government retaliate to the militants in the Red Mosque?

8. What did Operation Silence set off?

9. What was the one ray of hope? Why would citizens look forward to it?

10. What occurred on October 18, 2002?

11. What happened next?

12. On December 27 _____ was killed.

13. Why did Malala's father tell his daughter, "But just use him to learn the literal meaning of the words: don't follow his explanations and interpretations. Only learn what God says"?

CHAPTER 11

The Clever Class

1. Why did Malala find sanctuary in the school?

2. When not studying, how did the students spend their time?

3. What metaphor was used to describe day-to-day living in Swat?

4. What was the next threat from Fazlullah?

5. How did the family get through all of the bombings?

6. What was Quami Jirga?

7. What metaphor was used to describe Ziauddin's zeal in speaking on peace?

8. How is the state like a mother?

9. How did the poem by Martin Niemoller support Ziauddin's feeling at the time?

10. Why was Malala not afraid to speak out during interviews?

11. What was the simile used to describe the effectiveness of Malala's interviews?

12. Why were Sangota Convent School and Excelsior College destroyed?

13. Why was one of the worst times during Ramadan?

14. What was the announcement at the end of 2008?

CHAPTER 12

The Bloody Square

1. Who was Shabana and what happened to her?

2. Why did manual workers join the Taliban?

3. What atrocities occurred almost daily during Swat?

4. Why was it easier to recruit the poor as Taliban members?

5. Why did some think Ziauddin was a secret agent?

6. How was this period of time affecting the small children?

7. When does Talibanization become normal?

8. Summarize the conspiracy theories circulating during this time. Refer to page 151.

9. To what do the following statements refer: "...they were two sides of the same coin," and "we were caught like chaff between two stones of a water mill"?

10. Terror made people _____.

CHAPTER 13
The Diary of Gul Makai

1. Who was Gul Makai and what is the significance of the name?

2. Malala was informed about another famous diary writer. Who?

3. What was Malala's first entry about?

4. What evidence shows that Malala was defiant and determined?

5. How did Malala, aka Gul Makai, feel about the burqa?

6. How did Malala's behavior change as she was writing the diary?

7. What was the impact of the diary?

8. Why wasn't a hospital protected by the Taliban a good idea?

CHAPTER 14

A Funny Kind of Place

1. Why did Malala read Paulo Coelho's <u>The Alchemist</u> repeatedly?

2. Why did the Taliban reopen girls' schools to age 10?

3. What evidence shows that the truce of February 16, 2009 was a mirage?

4. Why was President Obama alarmed more about Pakistan than Afghanistan during this period of time?

5. What was Operation True Path?

CHAPTER 15

Leaving the Valley

1. Tradition tells the people of Swat only leave the valley for poverty or love, not because of the _____.

2. What are IDP's?

3. What simile was used to describe the busy exodus of families from Swat?

4. What did we know was not true?

5. Describe the Mardan refugee camps.

6. Why did Ziauddin leave the family?

7. How was Malala different from the other girls at school in Karshat?

8. Ziauddin and his family were living their own drama during this time. Explain.

PART THREE
Three Bullets, Three Girls

CHAPTER 16

The Valley of Sorrows

1. What was it like for the family returning to Swat after about three months?

2. "We people of Swat were first seduced by the Taliban, then killed by them and now _____ for them.

3. "In some ways, the army did not seem very different from the militants." Explain.

4. Why did Ziauddin's friends call it a "controlled peace, not a durable peace?"

5. After school was once again in session, some of the girls received a prized invitation. Explain.

6. While in Islamabad, the girls had many firsts. Explain.

7. How was Islamabad different from the village?

8. What did planting the mango seed in the garden during Ramadan represent?

9. How did General Abbas help solve Ziauddin's problem?

10. With all the changes, why were the villagers hard on the army?

11. How bad were the floods in 2010 in Pakistan? Give a comparison.

12. Why was this area called "the valley of sorrows"?

13. Explain theories as to why the devastation took place.

14. Why were foreign aid agencies fearful of their safety?

CHAPTER 17

Praying to Be Tall

1. Malala offered Allah a hundred *raakat nafl*. Explain.

2. Why would women often congregate at Malala's house?

3. The courts of Swat were busy with Blasphemy Law. What is it?

4. There were many complaints about America during this time. Explain.

5. What is the significance of the years, 1948, 1965, and 1971?

6. What were the mocking statements issued about the Americans sneaking into Pakistan undetected?

7. Malala was a busy young woman after October 2011. Explain.

8. Why wasn't Malala's parents completely happy with Malala being honored?

9. Malala made a lot of money during her public appearances. How did she spend it?

CHAPTER 18

The Woman and the Sea

1. What does it mean when the women want independence?

2. Malala and family went to Karachi as guests of Geo TV, naming a girls' secondary school in her honor. It is interesting to become familiar with Karachi. Read the following hyperlink.

   Karachi City
   www.karachi.com/v/economy/

3. The mohajirs all support a party called MQM. Refer to hyperlink.

   MQM
   www.mqm.org

4. Pashtuns are divided into the following parties. Refer to the hyperlinks.

   Imran Khan
   www.britannica.com/biography/Imran-Khan

   Maulana Fazlur Rehman
   http://en.wikipedia.org/wiki/Fazal-ur-Rehman_(politician)

   ANP-Pashtun Nationalist Party
   www.english.rfi.fr.asia-pacific/20130429-awami-national-party

PPP of Benazir Bhutto
www.history.com/topics/womens-history/benazir-bhutto

PML of Nawaz Sharif
www.pmin.org

5.	The family visited the mausoleum of their found and great leader Mohammad Ali Jinnah. Next to his tomb is that of Liaquat Ali Khan, their first prime minister.

Mohammad Jinnah
www.biography.com/people/mohammad-ali-jinnah-9354710

Liaquat Ali Khan
www.britannica.com/biography/liaquat-ali-khan

6.	Why was Malala confused by all the fighting?

7.	How did the threats arrive, and how did the family react to them.

CHAPTER 19

A Private Talibanization

1. What was the reaction of some in Swat to the girls' school trip to the White Palace?

2. Then strange things began happening. Explain.

3. On July 12, Malala turned fourteen. What did that mean?

4. The Taliban was creeping back into the area, but some how differently. Explain.

5. Who were to be the next two Taliban targets?

6. Why did Ziauddin refuse security?

7. How did Ziauddin take precautions?

CHAPTER 20
Who Is Malala?

1. Malala is superstitious and religious. Explain.

2. Malala was a good student. Explain.

3. Describe the scene of the ambush?

PART FOUR

Between Life and Death

CHAPTER 21

"God, I Entrust Her to You"

1. Where was Malala's mother and father when she was shot?

2. Why was Malala special to Ziauddin?

3. Who accompanied Ziauddin and Malala to the hospital and where did they go?

4. What were her injuries?

5. Why didn't the doctors operate immediately?

6. Why was Ziauddin irritated with all the people gathering at the hospital.

7. Malala's condition got worse. Explain.

8. What did her operation entail?

9. What did the two British doctors who were accidentally in Pakistan at the time discover about Malala's care?

10. What did Rehman Malik bring for Malala?

CHAPTER 22

Journey into the Unknown

1. By Thursday after she had been shot on Tuesday, Ziauddin was convinced that Malala would die. Explain.

2. What changes helped Malala survive?

3. Why was helping Malala a critical decision for Dr. Fiona?

4. How was security handled while Malala was hospitalized?

5. Not all reactions to the shooting were positive. Explain.

6. Why did Malala need to be moved again?

7. How and where did Malala go?

8. Why did Malala travel alone without her family?

PART FIVE
A Second Life

CHAPTER 23

"The Girl Shot in the Head, Birmingham"

1. What was the only thing Malala knew when she came around?

2. Malala's recovery was a slow process. Explain.

3. Besides recovering from her injuries, how did Malala feel when she woke up?

4. What issues was Malala concerned with when she tried to communicate?

5. When did Malala first show excitement while recovering?

6. What did Major General Ghulam Qamar mean when he said, "We are very happy our daughter has survived"?

7. Why was Ziauddin so angry?

8. What evidence shows that Malala was curious about how she looked?

9. Why can't people believe that a Muslim could attack me?

10. What did Malala's desperate mother threaten to do if arrangements could not be made for the family to leave?

11. How did Dr. Javid know that Malala's memory was fine?

12. What did Malala want from her parents when she learned they would be arriving in two days?

13. How did Malala pass the time in the hospital waiting for her parents to come?

14. Why wasn't Malala eating?

15. Who was the other Fiona?

16. Of all the gifts coming Malala's way, what were her favorites?

17. What was the global meaning of "I am Malala"?

CHAPTER 24

"They Have Snatched Her Smile"

1. How long had Malala and her family been separated?

2. Why did Ziauddin say, ". . .—they(Taliban) have snatched her smile"?

3. Explain the simile, "It was like a reverse mirror."

4. Who was Malala's attacker?

5. Who had unfairly been arrested?

6. More operations were to come. Explain.

7. How could Malala identify with Dorothy from the <u>The Wonderful Wizard of Oz?</u>

8. Where was Malala's first outing?

9. What were the reasons Malala was allowed to meet with Pakistan's president, Asif Zardari?

10. Why was meeting with President Zardari like a James Bond movie?

11. Why was the high commissioner told to give Ziauddin a post as education attache?

12. ". . .men and women chatting and mixing in a way that would be _____in Swat.

13. Why did Malala laugh at the warning not be out late on Broad Street on the weekend?

14. Who does Malala thank for her recovery?

EPILOGUE

One Child, One Teacher, One Book, One Pen. . .

1. Why was the rented family home called a sub-jail?

2. How was the family home in the UK different from Swat?

3. Describe in a short response how Malala's world has changed.

4. Respond to the following statement made by Malala's speech to the UN. "One child, one teacher, one book and one pen can change the world."

5. Why does Malala still campaign for the right of education for all? Use evidence from the text?

6. In and essay, respond to the following statement at the end of the book. "I am Malala. My world has changed but I have not". Organize your essay and support your main ideas with details from the book.

ANSWERS

I Am Malala

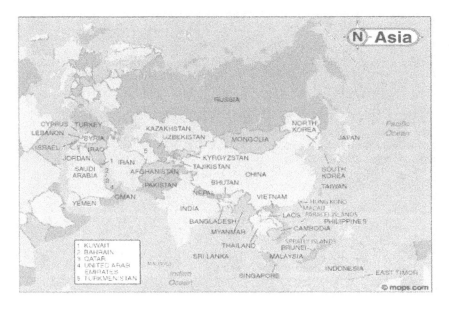

1. Locate Pakistan and all neighboring countries on this map of Asia.

2. Read the following article to familiarize yourself with the country of Pakistan.

   Pakistan Profile www.bbc.com/news/world-south-asia-12965779

3. Read the following article to familiarize yourself with the Taliban, past and present.

   The Taliban Today www.cfr.org/afghanistan/taliban-afghanistan/p10551

PROLOGUE
Prediction

1. Malala begins her story with this statement:

    I come from a country that was created at midnight. When I almost died it was just after midday.

    What do you think Malala meant by this statement?

    A.   Accept any reasonable answer.

2. What evidence is there that where Malala is now and where her story takes place is vastly different. Where is her home now?

    A.   Her life now has running water, hot and cold; electric lighting instead of oil lamps, convenient ovens; food in packets. She is now in Birmingham, England.

3. Malala and her girl friends attended school in secret. What is the evidence?

    A.   Malala's school had no sign because the Taliban thought girls should not go to school.

4. Behind closed doors, the mood was different. Explain.

    A.   They skipped through, casting off their headscarves to make way for the sun. A proud sign, Khushal School (founded by Malala's father), hung inside.

5. What evidence showed these girls took their education seriously?

    A. They attended school six days a week, chanted chemical equations, studying Urdu grammar, writing stories in English, and drawing diagrams of blood circulation.

6. In some ways Malala was like any other teenager. Explain.

    A. Like other teenagers, Malala liked to sleep in until lovingly awakened by her father and mother to get ready for school. She and her friends liked Justin Bieber songs and Twilight movies, had individual dreams: fashion designer, inventor, politician, teacher, doctor.

7. Malala excelled in school. Explain.

    A. She had awards hanging in her room for campaigning in her valley for peace and the right for girls to go to school.

8. The bus was a preferred mode of transportation over walking. Why?

    A. Walking was sweaty, lonely, and scary. The bus allowed her to chat with her friends, and her mother thought it safer since the Taliban had never come for a girl.

9. Describe the bus.

    A. *Dyna* was a white Toyota TownAce truck with three parallel benches, one along either side and one in the middle, carrying girls and teachers. Window frames were covered with yellowed, dusty thick plastic sheeting.

10. Describe Malala's injuries.

    A. One shot went through her left eye socket and out under her left shoulder. Two other shots hit her friends.

Part One
Before the Taliban

Rather I receive your bullet-riddled body with honor
Than news of your cowardice on the battlefield.

Traditional Pashto couplet

1. What do you think the above couplet means?

   A.   Accept any thought out answer.

CHAPTER 1

A Daughter is Born

Vocabulary

a. commiserated

b. auspicious

1. Culturally speaking, how are the births of girls and and boys celebrated?

    A. Rifles are fired in celebration of a son, while daughters are hidden away behind a curtain, their later roles to prepare food and give birth to children.

2. How is Malala's father different from most Pashtun men?

    A. He fell in love with his daughter at birth, foreseeing something different about her.

3. Describe the code of Pashtunwali.

    A. This code obliges hospitality to all and "honor" is the most important value. The worst thing a Pashtun can face is shame and loss of "face." Pashtuns fight among themselves but come together to fight outsiders trying to conquer their lands.

4. Our Malala is named after Malalai of Maiwand. Give a short summary of Malalai. Why is she compared to Joan of Arc?

A. **While in Britain, no one has heard of her, in Afghanistan Malalai (or Malala) is a legend. Smaller facts in the story vary slightly, but although it is Ayub Khan who became known as the Victor of Maiwand, it is said that it was Malalai who actually saved the day.**

    She was a native of Khig, a tiny village on the edge of the Maiwand battlefield, and the daughter of a shepherd. Both her father and fiancée joined with Ayub's army in the attack on the British on July 27th 1880 (which some say was also her wedding day), and like many women, Malalai was there to help tend to the wounded and provide water and spare weapons. Eventually there came a point in the battle where the Afghan army, despite their superior numbers, started to lose morale and the tide seemed to be turning in favour of the British. Seeing this, Malalai took off her veil and shouted out:

    "Young love! If you do not fall in the battle of Maiwand,
    By God, someone is saving you as a symbol of shame!"

    This gave many of the Afghan fighters and ghazis a new resolve and they redoubled their efforts. At that moment one of the leading flag-bearers fell from a British bullet, and Malalai went forward and held up the flag (some versions say she made a flag out of her veil), singing a landai:

    "With a drop of my sweetheart's blood,
    Shed in defense of the Motherland,
    Will I put a beauty spot on my forehead,
    Such as would put to shame the rose in the garden,"

    But then Malalai was herself struck down and killed. However, her words had spurred on her countrymen and soon the British lines gave way, broke and turned, leading to a disastrous retreat back to Kandahar and the biggest defeat for the Anglo-Indian army in the Second

Afghan War. Ayub Khan afterwards gave a special honour to Malalai and she was buried at her village, where her grave can still be found.

5. Why did Malala refer to her Swat Valley as the most beautiful place in the world?

   A. The "Welcome to Paradise" sign and reference to Switzerland of the East is due to the mountains, waterfalls, clear lakes. Swat serves as a ski resort and vacation spot for the rich and royalty.

6. Summarize the history of Swat by including independence of 1947, Mad Fakir, Mingora, and Buddhism to Islam.

   A. Answers should include Swat appeared autonomous while under the government of Pakistan following British giving India independence. Swat was surrounded by vast mountains where Malala's ancestors led by Mullah Saidullah, aka Mad Fakir battled British forces. Also although Islam has been part of Swat since the eleventh century, ancient ancestors were Buddhists since the second century as proven by archaeologists.

7. Malala valued her home in Swat. What evidence supports that fact?

   A. Family and friends gathered often on the roof of their one floor concrete house to play and have tea. Her valley was full of fruit trees. Malala's mother, while singing to birds, shared extra prepared food with neighboring hungry families. Malala loved to sit on her roof to dream. Like children in other countries that enjoy changing seasons, Malala and her friends made snowmen in the winter, watched the spring green, suffered from the hot and dry summer.

8. What purpose did a barber serve in the marriage of Malala's mother and father?

    A. Because Malala's grandfathers did not get along, the marriage between her mother and father was not welcome. The barber was used to send messages from Malala's father to his future bride's parents. After about nine months the marriage was granted.

9. Malala's father and mother do not share a traditional marriage. Explain

    A. Because Tor Pekai (Malala's mother) is a strong woman even though she cannot read or write, Malala's father shares everything with her, good and bad. Most Pashtun men believe this behavior is a male weakness. She is also very pious, praying five times a day. Praying in the mosque is only for men.

10. Why did Malala and her brother spend most of their time with their mother?

    A. Their father was gone most of the time, busy with school, literary societies, environmental issues, and village problems.

11. The sixteenth century proved to be devastating to the Yousafzai tribe (Malala's ancestors) in Pakistan and Afghanistan. Explain.

    A. The emperor was warned that the Yousafzai tribes were becoming powerful and would overthrow him. Six hundred chiefs were massacred, only two escaping.

12. Wesh was a strange system of land distribution among the tribesmen. Explain.

    A. Every five or ten years all families would swap villages and redistribute the land of the new village among the men so that everyone had the chance to work on good as well as band land. This arrangement was to keep rival clans from fighting.

13. Briefly describe the rule of King Miangul Abdul Wadood (Badshah Sahib) and his son Miangul Abdul Haq Jehanzeb.

   A. Badshah Sahib brought peace to the valley by building forts across the mountain and creating an army. He set up the first telephone and built the first primary school. His son built many schools, hospitals and roads. In 1969 this valley became part of Pakistan's North West Frontier Province.

14. Malala's father said of her daughter, "Malala will be free as a bird." Why did this mean so much in Pakistan?

   A. Although men and boys could roam freely about the town, women and girls could not go out without a male to accompany them. Malala, at an early age, knew she was not going to be like that.

CHAPTER 2

My father the Falcon

1. " . . my father had trouble with words." Explain

    A. **He was a stutterer at an early age, having trouble with m's, p's, and k's.**

2. What is the simile that describes grandfather Rohul Amin?

    A. **His rage was "like a hen going astray or a cup getting broken."**

3. How did Lewano Pir, Saint of the Mad, try to cure Malala's father of his stutter?

    A. **Pir spat into his open mouth. He also gave Malala's father some gur, dark molasses, rolled it around in his own mouth, took it out, and gave an amount to my grandmother to give a little to Ziauddin every day.**

4. What evidence shows that boys were valued more than girls in Pashtun families?

    A. **The boys went to school while the girls stayed home . . ."waitinging to be married". Males were given milk with their tea while the girls had straight tea. Eggs, when available, were given only to the boys. A slaughtered chicken was shared with both boys and girls, with the boys rewarded with luscious breast meat, while the girls ate the wings and neck.**

5. What was the impact of general Zia ul-Haq when he seized power in Pakistan? Include women's rights in court, madrasas, ISI, CIA, and Saudi Arabia.

    A. **He is most noted for his efforts to bring religion (Islamization) into mainstream society within Pakistan, and in foreign policy, for his close relationship with the United States and support for the mujahideen resistance against the Soviets in Afghanistan.**

    Zia ul-Haq reduced woman's evidence in court for only half that of a man's.

    Many madrasas, or religious schools, were opened during this time with rewritten history books describing Pakistan as a "fortress of Islam."

    The ISI, Pakistan's intelligence service helped train Afghan refugees as resistance fighters, or mujahideen.

    Pakistan became the main base for the CIA, bringing in billions of dollars and weapons to the area, helping to fight the communist Red Army.

    Saudi Arabia matched funds given to Pakistan by the United States.

6. Define jihad.

    A. **The Arabic word "jihad" is often translated as "holy war," but in a purely linguistic sense, the word " jihad" means struggling or striving.**

7. What are the five pillars of Islam?

    A. **The 'Five Pillars' of Islam are the foundation of Muslim life:**
        a. **Faith or belief in the Oneness of God and the finality of the prophethood of Muhammad**
        b. **Establishment of the daily prayers**

    c.   Concern for and almsgiving to the needy

    d.   Self-purification through fasting

    e.   The pilgrimage to Makkah or Mecca for those who are able.

8.   How did the CIA encourage jihad?

    A.   **United States had spent millions of dollars beginning in the 1980s to produce and disseminate anti-Soviet textbooks for Afghan schoolchildren. The books encouraged a jihadist outlook, which was useful propaganda at the time for a Washington driven by the imperatives of the Cold War.**

9.   Define maulana.

    A.   **Maulana is often the word of choice for addressing or referring to Muslim religious scholars that are respected.**

10.   "...years later the same maulana's organization would become the **Swat Taliban.**"

11.   How was the talib's instructions "a kind of brainwashing"?

    A.   **The talib told the young men of the villages that life was short with few opportunities except working in the mines or construction. Going to war between the Muslim and infidels became more important.**

12.   What was meant by the metaphor, "war between two elephants" and the simile, "like the grass crushed by the hooves to two fierce beasts"?

    A.   **The war in Afghanistan was really between the US and the Soviet Union (the war between two elephants) and the Pashtuns were the "grass crushed by the hooves to two fierce beasts".**

13. Why might it be difficult for some Pashtuns to have a birthday party?

   A. They remember years by events.

14. What evidence supports the fact that rivalry was significant in family dynamics?

   A. Pashtuns found it hard to "stomach" cousins becoming more popular, wealthier, or more influential. Malala's father was bullied by his cousins because of his dark skin. He could never do enough to please his father.

15. Who showed Malala's father his proud path?

   A. Malala's grandmother slipped him extra food at meals, made sure he studied, and gave him faith to travel his own path.

16. What evidence supports the frugality of Pashtuns?

   A. Malala's father was beaten for giving out bowls of maize to holy men. Malala's grandfather would fly into a rage if food was accidentally spilled onto the floor. His frugality became embarrassing when Malala's father was forced to apply for teaching rebates and use recycled textbooks from previous students.

17. What was Baba's (grandfather) greatest gift to Malala's father?

   A. The gift of education, love for learning, and an awareness of people's rights.

18. What were the results of Malala's father first speech as a boy?

   A. After committing the speech written by his father to memory and practicing, he gave a flawless presentation, ending his stuttering. He also made his father smile. He then entered every competition in the district. He was called a shaheen or falcon, a creature that flies high above other birds.

CHAPTER 3

Growing Up in a School

1. Why was Malala's mother unusual in the village as a child?

    A. She was actually encouraged to go to school. At six years old she was in a class, the only girl. She envied her girl cousins at home playing. She saw no point in going to school since she would just end up cooking, cleaning, and bringing up children.

2. Why was education important to Malala's father?

    A. He loved reading books. His ambition was to open his own school. He valued schooling because his sisters did not have the opportunity. He believed lack of education was the root of Pakistan's problems. He wanted schooling available for all, rich and poor, girls and boys.

3. What obstacles did Ziauddin face trying to realize his dream?

    A. Baba wanted Ziauddin to become a doctor, a much more lucrative career. Teachers were poor providers. Baba refused to pay for Ziauddin's living expenses. He had no place to stay.

4. Pakistan has a class system. Explain.

    A. The people in Sewoor (Gujars, Kohistanis, and Mians) were treated differently. The Mians were landowners, while the Gujars, Kohistanis were hilly peasants who looked after the buffalo. Even the poor Pashtuns would say, "They are dirty, black and stupid. Let them be illiterate."

5. How did Ziauddin's fate change?

    A. His new brother-in-law, Nasir Pacha, liked the hilly people and respected their hard lives. He offered his home in Spal Bandi to Ziauddin while he went to school.

6. Why were Akbar Khan and Nasir Pacha important to Ziauddin?

    A. He learned the concept that if you help someone in need you might also receive unexpected aid.

7. How did Pakistan change when Benazir Bhutto became prime minister?

    A. She was the first female prime minister and the first in the Islamic world. This created optimism about the future. Student political organizations became active.

8. Explain The Satanic Verse by Salman Rushdie

    A. *The Satanic Verses* controversy, also known as the Rushdie Affair, was the heated and frequently violent reaction of Muslims to the publication of Salman Rushdie's novel *The Satanic Verses*, which was first published in the United Kingdom in 1988. Many Muslims accused Rushdie of blasphemy or unbelief and in 1989 Ayatollah Khomeini of Iran issued a fatwa ordering Muslims to kill Rushdie. Numerous killings, attempted killings, and bombings resulted from Muslim anger over the novel.

9. Why was it important for Malala's father to start his own school?

    A. Small private colleges paid very little money and Ziauddin was expected to contribute to the household. He longed for the freedom of running his own school, encouraging independent thought, open-mindedness, and creativity.

10. Running a school is like running any other business. Explain.

A. A school requires a big outlay of money. Tuition demands need to equal expenses. Business partners should be able to work together. Because Pashtuns value hospitality, they now had a place for everyone knocking on their doors to stay—for free. Besides opening the door for students, there needs to be money to equip the schools. When Ziauddin tried to register the school, he faced ridicule from the officials anticipating bribes in the form of money and lavish meals.

11. Why did Ziauddin become a spokesman for others in education?

A. He could not agree with paying bribes, "running a school is not a crime." He became president of an organization of 400 principals, arguing the officials were the servants and we teach their children.

12. Why is a small boy brought into a marriage ceremony to sit on the laps of the bride and groom?

A. This encourages the birth of a son.

13. And then . . ."when it seem matters could not get worse, the area was hit by **flash floods**.

14. When did their luck change?

A. Hidayatullah said, "Malala was a lucky girl. When she was born our luck changed."

15. **9/11** would change their world, and bring war into our valley

CHAPTER 4

The Village

1. What is "woma"?

    A. Woma means seventh and is a celebration of day seven in a newborn's life. Family and friends attend.

2. Describe the Eid holidays.

    A. Eid occurs twice a year, Eid ul-Fitr marks the end of Ramadan fasting month, and Eid ul-Azha commemorates the Prophet Abraham's readiness to sacrifice his son Ismail to God. This celebration took us on a five hour ride to the mountain of Shangla with rope bridges and pulley system.

3. Contrast city life in Mingora and out in the Shangla valley.

    A. In Shangla people grew radishes and walnut trees and bee hives. Water buffalo gathered at the river with a wooden waterwheel providing power to turn huge millstones to grind wheat and maize into flour, which young boys would then pour into sacks. The soil was rich and butterflies flew about. Houses were made of wattle and daub (a composite building material used for making walls, in which a woven lattice of wooden strips called wattle is daubed with a sticky material usually made of some combination of wet soil, clay, sand, animal dung and straw). There were no hospitals, and politicians only

visited during election time. The night would be lit by
oil lamps in the houses. The women would tell stories.
Women from the village had their faces covered when
they left their quarters and could not meet or speak to
men who were not close relatives.

4.   Why does Malala question the Pashtun code of conduct?

    A.   Girls are sold to older men simply because they may
want a younger wife. One girl was poisoned by her own
family when she looked at a boy (flirting). A girl can be
given to another tribe to settle a feud. Nobody can
marry a widow without the family's permission.

5.   How were women in Afghanistan treated?

    A.   Women had to wear burqas, with only a grilles to look
out of. The Taliban banned women from laughing out
loud or wearing white shoes, because white was for
men. Women were locked up for wearing nail polish.

6.   "For me the valley was a sunny place and I couldn't see the clouds
gathering behind the mountains" is a metaphor for what?

    A.   The Taliban were right around the corner and they
were Pashtun like Malala.

CHAPTER 5

Why I Don't Wear Earrings and
Pashtuns Don't Say Thank You

1. How did Malala react when the new girl, Malka-e-Noor came in first in end-of-year exams?

   A. **She cried and was comforted by her mother.**

2. Malala was not a perfect child. Explain.

   A. **She started stealing from her friend Safina who had stolen her favorite toy. This became compulsive behavior for Malala. Made to face her actions taught her not to steal or lie. She doesn't wear jewelry so she is not tempted to steal.**

3. How did Ziauddin react to Malala's behavior?

   A. **He told her about mistakes that heroes made when they were children. Mahatma Gandhi said, "Freedom is not worth having if it does not include the freedom to make mistakes."**

4. Why does Malala have a problem with the Pashtunwali code?

   A. **Pashtunwali code calls for revenge for wrongs done to us. Where does this end?**

5.   Why do Pashtuns not say "thank you"?

   A.   Because Pashtuns never forget a good deed, they will reciprocate at some point.

6.   Why is Malala inspired by Khan Abdul Ghaffar Khan?

   A.   He believes in a non-violent philosophy to the culture.

7.   Why were the people of Swat subservient to the new regimes?

   A.   Criticism was not tolerated. Offenses were punished by entire families being expelled from Swat.

8.   How did Malala try to win back her father's respect?

   A.   Malala entered a public speaking competition with the topic, "Honesty is the best policy."

9.   Whom do these quotes belong: "It is far more honorable to fail than to cheat" and "teach him how to gracefully lose"?

   A.   Abraham Lincoln.

10.   What were the results of the speech competition?

   A.   Malala came in second to her friend Moniba. She decided in the future she would do better if she would tell her own story, so she started writing her own speeches and delivering them from the heart instead of a sheet of paper.

CHAPTER 6

Children of the Rubbish Mountain

1. What was Malala's favorite TV show? Why?

   A."Shaka Laka Boom Boom" was about a boy, Sanju, who had a magic pencil. Everything he drew became real. Malala wanted this magic for herself. She wanted to help the kids in the rubbish mountain.

2. Helping poor families with tuition was controversial. Why?

   A.
   - Ziauddin was giving away at least 100 free places in his school which cut greatly into operating money.
   - Some of these poor students came to Malala's house in the morning to have breakfast.
   - Other paying parents took their children out of the school because they thought it was shameful that their children shared the classroom with children of the people who cleaned their houses.
   - Having so many other people around made it hard for Malala to study.
   - The rubbish children were breadwinners so if they went to school the whole family would go hungry.

3. Translate: "Kia hasool e elum in bachun ka haq nahe" What is its significance?

    A. "Is education not the right of these children?" This was posted on thousands of leaflets and left around the town.

4. How did the army feel about Ziauddin becoming a known figure in Swat?

    A. A local commander called him "lethal" in public.

5. What are "ghost schools"?

    A. Influential people with money took money from the government to start schools but had no pupils. Their buildings were used for other things.

6. Aside from corruption and bad government, my father's main concern in those days was the **environment**.

7. 9/11 changed the world but how did it affect Swat?

    A. Swat was at the epicenter. Osama bin Laden had been living in Kandahar when the attack of the World Trade Center occurred. American sent thousands of troops. ISI had created the Taliban with shared beliefs.

8. How did the citizens of Swat feel about the Taliban?

    A. They were not fans because the Taliban had destroyed girls' schools and blew up giant Buddha statues. But many Pakistanis did not like the bombing of Afghanistan and how Pakistan was helping Americans crossing their airspace. Some religious leaders saw Osama bin Laden as a hero. Conspiracy theories began about the attack being carried out by Jews as an excuse for America to launch a war on the Muslim world. Some 12,000 young men from Swat went to help the Taliban.

9. Musharraf was double-dealing. How?

   A. He was taking money from America while still helping the jihadis.

10. What measures did Malala take to help the rubbish children?

    A. She wrote a letter to God even though she didn't know how to get the letter to him.

CHAPTER 7

The Mufti Who Tried to Close Our School

1. What was meant by Ziauddin's dialogue, "That maulana has a bad eye on us."?

    A. The self-proclaimed maulana across from where Malala grew up was watching the success of the school, the girls going in and out. He wanted the woman owner to close the school and rent it to him.

2. What evidence supports not all Muslims think the same?

    A. There are many strands of Islam in Pakistan. The founder, Jinnah wanted a land of tolerance, the rights of Muslims in India to be recognized. The feud between the Muslims and Hindus resulted in millions of deaths.

3. ". . .Muslims are split between **Sunnis** and **Shias**. What is the implication?

    A. Both sects share the same fundamental beliefs and and same Holy Quran, but disagree over who was the right person to lead the religion when the Prophet died in the seventh century. Although 80% of Pakistan are Sunnis, they, too, are divided into many subsects.

5. The mufi across the street was a member of of Tablighi Jamaat, a Deobandi group. Why is this important to the story?

   A. The Deobandi group are very conservative and most of the madrasas were this sect.

6. How was the controversy about the school solved?

   A. Ziauddin compromised by saying he would have the girls enter the school through another gate.

7. How did the mufti feel about the women?

   A. Hel felt all women must observe purdah. (the practice among women in certain Muslim and Hindu societies of living in a separate room or behind a curtain, or of dressing in all-enveloping clothes, in order to stay out of the sight of men or strangers)

8. How was General Musharrah different from General Zia?

   A.
   - **General Musharraf called himself chief executive instead of chief martial law administrator.**
   - **He kept dogs, which Muslims thought unclean.**
   - **He opened up media allowing new TV channels with female newsreaders, and dancing on TV.**
   - **He changed the rape laws not requiring women to have four male witnesses.**
   - **He appointed first woman governor of the state bank, women airline pilots, and women to the coastguard.**

9. How were things different in Swat?

   A. Swat was controlled by MMA or as some jokingly called it, Mullah Military Alliance. The Taliban was trained in some of the local madrasas.

10. What was the Arabization of Pakistan?

    A. **During Afghan jihad, Saudi money funded many madrasas.**

11. How did MMA affect Swat?

    A.
      - **They banned CD and DVD shops.**
      - **Launched attacks on cinemas**
      - **Tore down billboards with pictures of women blacked out with paint**
      - **They harassed women for wearing Western style shirts and trousers instead of traditional wear**
      - **After 2004 climate changed so that boys and girls could not be in the same class.**

12. What is FATA and its significance?

    A. **FATA translates to Federally Administrated Tribal Areas. After 2004 Musharraf, with urging from Washington, sent an army to search al-Qaeda using the area as a safe haven, taking advantage of the Pashtun hospitality.**

13. What were tribal agencies like?

    A. **They are forgotten places of harsh rocky valleys, few schools and hospitals, where few women can read, known for fierceness and independence.**

14. What was the result of the army entering tribal areas in March 2004?

    A. **Local people saw this as an attack. Since tribal men carry weapons, hundreds of soldiers were killed. The army pulled back and called a negotiated peace settlement with tribal leader, Nek Mohammad.**

15. What happened June 17, 2004?

    A. Nek Mohammad and those around him were attacked by a US drone.

16. Why were local people shocked?

    A. Locals were angry and confused because they were not at war with Americans. Then there were more attacks.

CHAPTER 8

The Autumn of the Earthquake

1. How devastating was the earthquake of October 5, 2007?

    A.

    - **The earthquake affected 30,000 sq. km., an area as big as Connecticut.**
    - **It registered 7.6 on the Richter Scale.**
    - **More than 73,000 people were killed, 128,000 injured.**
    - **Approximately three and a half million people lost their homes.**
    - **Roads, bridges, water and power were gone.**
    - **6,400 school destroyed while 18,000 children lost their lives**

2. Where did aid come from?

    A.

    - **First TNSM (Movement for the Enforcement of Islamic Law).**
    - **Americans sent in supplies.**
    - **Islamic charities and organizations**
    - **ronts for militant groups like Jamaat-ul-Dawa (JuD) set up relief camps patrolled by men with Kalashnikovs and walkie-talkies.**

3. How would you summarize the JuD and their actions after the earthquake?

    A.   Accept any reasonable answer.

PART TWO

The Valley of Death

CHAPTER 9
Radio Mullah

1. The Taliban came to the alley led by <u>Maulana Fazlullah</u>.

    <u>The Iron Fist of Maulana Fazlullah</u>

    <u>Maulana Fazlullah</u>

2. Describe the men of the Taliban.

    A.
    - **strange looking men with long straggly hair and beards**
    - **camouflage vests over the shalwar kamiz worn with trousers well above the ankle**
    - **jogging shoes or cheap plastic sandals**
    - **some had stockings over their heads with holes for their eyes**
    - **black badges that said, "Sharia Law" or "Martyrdom"**
    - **some wore black turbans**
    - **called the Black Turbaned Brigade**

3. How did Fazlullah communicate with the valley?

    A. He set up an illegal radio station known as Mullah FM.

4. How did Fazlullah appear wise to those in the valley?

    A.
    - **He said he was an Islamic reformer and interpreter.**
    - **Encouraged people to adopt good habits**
    - **His voice seemed reasonable.**
    - **He wept when he spoke his love for Islam.**
    - **Convened local court**
    - **Local disputes were now handled quickly.**

5. What behaviors was Fazlullah attempting to enforce?

    A.
    - **Stop listening to music, watching TV, dancing**
    - **Denounced Pakistani government officials as infidels**
    - **Injustice of the feudal system (Khans)**
    - **Women are to fulfill their responsibilities at home and only go out in emergencies.**
    - **Closed beauty shops**
    - **Women were not to go to bazaars.**
    - **Stopped polio vaccine**

6. Mullahs misinterpreted the Quran and Hadith. Explain.

    A.   Because few people understood original Arabic, Fazlullah exploited their ignorance by saying it meant something different.

7. How do the militants gain support?

    A.   They first won the hearts of people by targeting those responsible for local problems. By doing this they gained support of the silent majority.

8. Who were the Falcon Commandos?

    A.   Volunteer traffic police who drove through the streets with machine guns mounted on their pickup trucks

9.   Fazlullah became more aggressive. Explain.

A.   They began killing khans and political activists.

10.   What message was taped to the school gate after the family arrived back home from Eid?

A.". . . the school you are running is Western and infidel. You teach girls and have a uniform that is un-Islamic."

11.   What is the meaning of "you have put the first stone in standing water. Now we will have the courage to speak"?

A.   Because Ziauddin took the first step to speaking against the militants, other citizens now had the courage to speak their minds.

CHAPTER 10

Toffees, Tennis Balls and the Buddhas of Swat

1. When the Taliban destroyed the thousand Buddhas, they were doing more damage than smashing statues. Explain.

   A. They were destroying history, Swat's special story. They became the enemy of fine arts, cultures, and history.

2. When Fazlullah came to Swat, there were no more school trips. Why?

   A. Girls were not supposed to be seen outside.

3. How did Malala feel about the Taliban telling everyone what to do and how to dress?

   A. She voiced her displeasure by saying, "I thought if God wanted us to be like that, he wouldn't have made us all different.

4. Why did noone do anything when the Taliban attacked the police in the valley?

   A. People seemed to be in a trance, seduced by propaganda.

5. Why had the whole country gone mad?

A. The Taliban had moved into Pakistan's capital, Islamabad.

6. What does, "when it suits the Taliban, women can be vocal and visible" mean?

A. Young women from the Red Mosque's female madrasa attacked CD and DVD shops with sticks. Umme Hassan trained many of the girls to become suicide bombers.

7. How did the government retaliate to the militants in the Red Mosque?

A. Tanks and armored personnel carriers surrounded the mosque, cutting off electricity and calling for the girls to surrender.

8. What did Operation Silence set off.

A. Fazlullah declared war on the Pakistani government. Now he could carry out his threats and mobilize support in the name of Lal Masjid.

9. What was the one ray of hope? Why would citizens look forward to it?

A. Benazir Bhutto was returning. Girls could think and speak out, and become politicians. She symbolized an end to dictatorship, a message of hope to the rest of the world. She openly spoke out against militants and offered help to Americans to find bin Laden.

10. What occurred on October 18, 2002?

A. Militants carried out an attempted assassination of Benazir.

11. What happened next?

     **A. Musharraf sent thousands of troops into the valley, cur-
     fews taking over citizens' lives.**

12. On December 27 **Benazir** was killed.

13. Why did Malala's father tell his daughter, "But just use him to
     learn the literal meaning of the words: don't follow his explana-
     tions and interpretations. Only learn what God says"?

     **A. When Malala's quari shaibs (Islamic studies' teacher)
     tried to justify Benazir's assassination, she was shocked.
     But her father told her they needed him to learn the
     Quran.**

CHAPTER 11

The Clever Class

1. Why did Malala find sanctuary in the school?

    A.   While in the street, she thought every man was a Talib. Students had to smuggle bags and books.

2. When not studying, how did the students spend their time?

    A.   The girls wrote and performed plays.

3. What metaphor was used to describe day-to-day living in Swat?

    A.   Malala said, "If there is a snake and a lion coming to attack us, what would we say is good, the snake or lion?"

4. What was the next threat from Fazlullah?

    A.   Fazlullah and his militants began blowing up schools in 2008.

5. How did the family get through all of the bombings?

    A.   The family felt fear at night but that was outweighed by courage to rid the village of the Taliban.

6. What was Quami Jirga?

    A. Quami Jirga was an assembly formed by elders in Swat to challenge Fazlullah, Ziauddin being the spokesperson.

7. What metaphor was used to describe Ziauddin's zeal in speaking on peace?

    A. He compared current conflict go going to the doctor with a headache but telling him you had a stomach ache. You must speak the truth.

8. How is the state like a mother?

    A. The state is like a mother because a mother never deserts her children.

9. How did the poem by Martin Niemoller support Ziauddin's feeling at the time?

    A. He hated that people kept quiet. With silence, nothing would change.

10. Why was Malala not afraid to speak out during interviews?

    A.". . . was the belief God would protect me."

11. What was the simile used to describe the effectiveness of Malala's interviews?

    A.". . .words were like eucalyptus blossoms of spring tossed away on the wind." Schools were still being destroyed.

12. Why were Sangota Convent School and Excelsior College destroyed?

    A. The Kahn said Sangota school was a school teaching Christianity, and Excelsior School was coeducational. Both statements were false, however.

13. Why was one of the worst times during Ramadan?

    A.   The Taliban bombed the power station and gas pipeline making it difficult to feed the families. There was no clean water either.

14. What was the announcement at the end of 2008?

    A.   As of January 15 all girls' schools would be closed.

CHAPTER 12

The Bloody Square

1. Who was Shabana and what happened to her?

   A. She was a dancer and was shot to death for performing.

2. Why did manual workers join the Taliban?

   A. Although they made great contributions to Pashtun society, they received no recognition or respect. Joining the Taliban gave them status and power.

3. What atrocities occurred almost daily during Swat?

   A. Bombings, public whippings, hangings, and beheadings were carried out by Taliban.

4. Why was it easier to recruit the poor as Taliban members?

   A. The rich could flee, but the poor were forced to stay and survive the best they could.

5. Why did some think Ziauddin was a secret agent?

   A. He was so outspoken but still alive.

6. How was this period of time affecting the small children?

    A. With so many killings, it seemed natural for little ones to think of coffins and graves. Instead of hide-and-seek and cops and robbers, children played army against the Taliban-sports of terror.

7. When does Talibanization become normal?

    A. When the highest authority in your district joins the Taliban, Talibanization becomes normal.

8. Summarize the conspiracy theories circulating during this time. Refer to page 151.

    A. Accept any reasonable answer.

9. To what do the following statements refer: ". . .they were two sides of the same coin," and "we were caught like chaff between two stones of a water mill"?

    A.
    Both army and the Taliban were powerful.
    Both set up roadblocks.
    Both would stop the local people.

10. Terror made people **<u>cruel</u>**.

CHAPTER 13
The Diary of Gul Makai

1. Who was Gul Makai and what is the significance of the name?

    A. Gul Makai was the pseudonym of Malala, used because no one would recognize her while giving public interviews. The name, "Gul Makai," means cornflower.

2. Malala was informed about another famous diary writer. Who?

    A. Hai Kabar told Malala about Anne Frank and how she kept a diary of her time hidden in Amsterdam during WWII.

3. What was Malala's first entry about?

    A."I Am Afraid" was the first entry about a dream she had about being afraid to go to school because of the Taliban edict.

4. What evidence shows that Malala was defiant, and determined?

    A. She wore a pink dress to school when told by the Taliban, "Do not wear colorful clothes."

5. How did Malala, aka Gul Makai, feel about the burqa?

   A. As a child, one loves the burqa because it's like dressing up, but that feeling changes as an adult. Walking is difficult in the burqa and suspicious business owners thought women dressed in burqas were suicide bombers.

6. How did Malala's behavior change as she was writing the diary?

   A. Her shyness turned to confidence.

7. What was the impact of the diary?

   A. Malala began to see the power of words.

8. Why wasn't a hospital protected by the Taliban a good idea?

   A. Ziauddin told Azul, "Don't accept good things from bad people."

CHAPTER 14

A Funny Kind of Place

1.   Why did Malala read Paulo Coelho's <u>The Alchemist</u> repeatedly?

    A.   Because it says, "When you want something all the universe conspires in helping you achieve it."

2.   Why did the Taliban reopen girls' schools to age 10?

    A.   The Taliban reopened them due to public outcry, even Pakistani media.

3.   What evidence shows that the truce of February 16, 2009 was a mirage?

    A.
- **Just two days later a TV reporter had been killed after covering a peace march led by Sufi Mohammad.**
- **Taliban were now state-sanctioned terrorists.**
- **They were still patrolling the Cheena Bazaar.**
- **Video were filmed flogging of teenage girls.**
- **". . .we are coming to Islamabad," Sufi Mohammad said.**
- **Taliban streamed into Bruner and did what they had done in Swat.**

4. Why was President Obama alarmed more about Pakistan than Afghanistan during this period of time?

    A. Pakistan had more than 200 nuclear warheads and the United States was concerned who was going to control them.

5. What was Operation True Path?

    A. It was an attempt to drive out the Taliban from the villages, urging all to leave.

CHAPTER 15

Leaving the Valley

1. Tradition tells the people of Swat only leave the valley for poverty or love, not because of the **Taliban**.

2. What are IDP's?

   A. **The families of the area became IDP's, internally displaced persons.**

3. What simile was used to describe the busy exodus of families from Swat?

   A."It was as though we are the Israelites leaving Egypt, but we have no Moses to guide us.

4. What did we know was not true?

   A."In a few days we will return."

5. Describe the Mardan refugee camps.

   A.
   - **More than two million people left Swat, more than could be housed in the tents.**
   - **Very hot inside the tents**
   - **There was talk of cholera spreading inside the tents.**
   - **There were rumors of the Taliban harassing the women.**

6. Why did Ziauddin leave the family?

   A. He felt he needed to warn the people of Peshawar and Islamabad to be aware of the conditions the IDP's were living and that the military were doing nothing.

7. How was Malala different from the other girls at school in Karshat?

   A. She didn't cover her face, she talked to every teacher and asked questions.

8. Ziauddin and his family were living their own drama during this time. Explain.

   A. They stayed for awhile with their family in Shangla for about six weeks. Next they traveled to Peshawar to meet Ziauddin. The whole family traveled to Islamabad, staying with friends. We, then, went to Abbottabad after Malala did an interview for a radio station called Power 99. Finally, Malala spent her twelfth birthday in Haripur.

PART THREE

Three Bullets, Three Girls

CHAPTER 16

The Valley of Sorrows

1. What was it like for the family returning to Swat after about three months?

   A.
   - **Army checkpoints everywhere**
   - **Building in ruins and burned-out vehicles**
   - **Walls riddled with bullet holes**
   - **Silent and empty**
   - **Looting prevalent**
   - **Our school had become a battlefield.**

2. "We people of Swat were first seduced by the Taliban, then killed by them and now **blamed** for them.

3. "In some ways, the army did not seem very different from the militants." Explain.

   A.
   - **Bodies of dead Taliban were left in the streets for all to see.**
   - **Young children were being arrested and sent to special camp for jihadis to de-radicalize them.**

4. Why did Ziauddin's friends call it a "controlled peace, not a durable peace?

    A. Many of the Taliban was were in hiding, not captured, so it was only a matter of time they would return to power.

5. After school was once again in session, some of the girls received a prized invitation. Explain.

    A. Their friend Shiza Shahid from Islamabad had finished her studies and invited twenty-seven girls from Kushal to spend a few days in the capital seeing sights and attending workshops to get relief from the trauma of living under the Taliban.

6. While in Islamabad, the girls had many firsts. Explain.

    A.
    - **Visited the Faisal Mosque**
    - **Attended the theater**
    - **Had art classes**
    - **Ate at McDonalds**

7. How was Islamabad different from the village?

    A.
    - **Islamabad had women lawyers, doctors, and activists that maintained their culture.**
    - **Women without purdah, with heads completely uncovered.**
    - **Army headquarters had green lawns and flowers in bloom.**

8. What did planting the mango seed in the garden during Ramadan represent?

    A. Planting the seed represented hope.

9. How did General Abbas help solve Ziauddin's problem?

   A. **Because the family had been gone for some time, he had collected no fees to help with school expenses, so the teachers had not been paid. Upon request, General Abbas sent Ziauddin 1,100,000 rupees. Ziauddin had enough to pay the teachers for three months.**

10. With all the changes, why were the villagers hard on the army?

    A. **The army had not caught any of the Taliban leadership. Because of that, there were still skirmishes and suicide attacks.**

11. How bad were the floods in 2010 in Pakistan? Give a comparison.

    A. **More lives had been affected and more damage had been caused by the floods than the Asian tsunami, the 2005 earthquake, Hurricane Katrina and the Haiti earthquake combined.**

12. Why was this area called "the valley of sorrows"?

    A. **First the earthquake, then the Taliban, then the military operation, and now, the floods**

13. Explain theories as to why the devastation took place.

    A. **Environmentalists warned that the mountains has been stripped of trees by the Taliban and timber smugglers. Some thought that the Americans using HAARP (High Frequency Active Auroral Research Program) technology, which causes huge waves under the ocean, thus flooding the land.**

14. Why were foreign aid agencies fearful of their safety?

    A. **The Taliban demanded officials reject any help from Christians and Jews.**

CHAPTER 17

Praying to Be Tall

1. Malala offered Allah a hundred *raakat nafl.* Explain.

    A. **Raakat nafl are extra voluntary prayers on top of the five daily ones if he would give her a little more height.**

2. Why would women often congregate at Malala's house?

    A. **Men were going missing, picked up by the army or ISI. Because Ziauddin is the spokesman for the Swat Qaumi Jirga, he acts as a liaison between the people and the army.**

3. The courts of Swat were busy with Blasphemy Law. What is it?

    A. **The Blasphemy Law protects the Holy Quran. Anyone who defiles the name of the Holy Prophet can be punished by death. Asia Bibi, a Christian, was sentenced to death. Salman Taseer shot down in the street for trying to help her.**

4. There were many complaints about America during this time. Explain.

    A.
     - **Drone attacks were killing civilians weekly.**
     - **CIA agent, Raymond Davis, killed two men in Lahore, said to be a spy by many.**

- Blood money amounting to $2.3 million was paid and Davis left the country.
- After Davis left, another done attacked tribal council killing forty people.
- Navy Seals seemed oblivious to the location of bin Laden but did kill him, alone, no help from allies.

5. What is the significance of the years, 1948, 1965, and 1971?

   A. **They were years of war with India.**

6. What were the mocking statements issued about the Americans sneaking into Pakistan undetected?

   A. **"Please don't honk, the army is sleeping," and "second-Hand Pakistani radar for sale. . .can't detect US helicopters but gets TV cable just fine."**

7. Malala was a busy young woman after October 2011. Explain.

   A.
   - **She was one of five nominees for the International Peace Prize of KidsRights, a children's advocacy group based in Amsterdam.**
   - **She was invited to speak in Lahore at an education gala, receiving $4,500 for her campaign on girls' rights.**
   - **She won the Pakistan's National Peace Prize, presenting the prime minister a list of educational demands.**

8. Why wasn't Malala's parents completely happy with Malala being honored?

   A. **Pakistan culture does not honor people while they are alive. Could this be a bad omen? Malala's mother thought her daughter might become a target. "I don't want awards, I want my daughter."**

9.   Malala made a lot of money during her public appearances. How did she spend it?

A.
- **The money had little meaning to her. She had a war to win.**
- **She did get a new bed and cabinet for her room.**
- **Malala's mother received tooth implants.**
- **The family purchased land in Shangla.**
- **The rest was spent on people who needed help.**
- **Malala started an education fund, focusing on girls from the street.**

CHAPTER 18
The Woman and the Sea

1. What does it mean when the women want independence?

    A.
    - **They want to make decisions for themselves.**
    - **They want to be free to go to school or go to work.**
    - **They do not want to be dependent on men.**

2. Malala and family went to Karachi as guests of Geo TV, naming a girls' secondary school in her honor. It is interesting to become familiar with Karachi. Read the following hyperlink.

    Karachi City

3. The mohajirs all support a party called MQM. Refer to hyperlink.

    MQM

4. Pashtuns are divided into the following parties. Refer to the hyperlinks.

    Imran Khan

    Maulana Fazlur Rehman

    ANP-Pashtun Nationalist Party

PPP of Benazir Bhutto

PML of Nawaz Sharif

5. The family visited the mausoleum of their found and great leader Mohammad Ali Jinnah. Next to his tomb is that of Liaquat Ali Khan, their first prime minister.

Mohammad Jinnah

Liaquat Ali Khan

6. Why was Malala confused by all the fighting?

    A. If Christians, HIndus, or Jews are really the enemy of Muslims, then why are they (Muslims) fighting among themselves. The focus should be on practical issues; illiterate people, women who have no education at all, bombed schools, no reliable electricity supply.

7. How did the threats arrive, and how did the family react to them.

    A.
    - **A Pakistani journalist, Shehla Njum from Alaska told the family that the Taliban had issued threats.**
    - **Malala's parents wanted her to stop campaigning and go into hiding.**
    - **Malala was not afraid of death, and wanted to continue campaigning for "something bigger than our lives".**

CHAPTER 19

A Private Talibanization

1. What was the reaction of some in Swat to the girls' school trip to the White Palace?

   A. Photocopied letters were distributed to many about the girls' "vulgar and obscene" behavior while on their trip.

2. Then strange things began happening. Explain.

   A.
   - **Strangers came and asked questions about the family.**
   - **Men from the intelligence service argued about the painting competition.**
   - **The family was questioned about distributing clothes to the poor.**

3. On July 12, Malala turned fourteen. What did that mean?

   A. She was considered an adult.

4. The Taliban was creeping back into the area, but some how differently. Explain.

   A. The Taliban was issuing specific threats instead of general threats and changing the mentality of people.

5. Who were to be the next two Taliban targets?

    A. Ziauddin and his friend, Zahid Kahn, were targeted.

6. Why did Ziauddin refuse security?

    A. He felt if he had security, then the Taliban would hit with more fire power and many more people could be killed.

7. How did Ziauddin take precautions?

    A. He changed his daily routine.

CHAPTER 20

Who Is Malala?

1. Malala is superstitious and religious. Explain.

   A. **Giving cooked rice to the poor, even the ants and birds will pray for them. Malala would say the Ayat al-Kursi, the Verse of the Throne seven times, five times would keep all safe from the devils. Malala prayed to Allah for high marks on her exams.**

2. Malala was a good student. Explain.

   A.
   - **Exams gave her a chance to show off.**
   - **She was competitive, wanting the top score.**
   - **She loved physics because it about truth.**
   - **She reread the entire textbook the night before the exams.**

3. Describe the scene of the ambush?

   A. **Accept any reasonable summary.**

PART FOUR

Between Life and Death

CHAPTER 21

"God, I Entrust Her to You"

1. Where was Malala's mother and father when she was shot?

    A. **He was giving a speech at the Swat Press Club for a meeting of the Association of Private Schools. Malala's mother was getting her own reading lesson at that time.**

2. Why was Malala special to Ziauddin?

    A. **Malala was Ziauddin's comrade in arm, first as Gul Makai, then openly as Malala.**

3. Who accompanied Ziauddin and Malala to the hospital and where did they go?

    A. **Madam Maryam, she was like a second mother to Malala. The left by helicopter to CMH (Combined Military Hospital) in Peshawar.**

4. What were her injuries?

    A. **The bullet went into her forehead and then traveled to her shoulder, lying next to her shoulder blade.**

5. Why didn't the doctors operate immediately?

    A. **The bullet had traveled close to the brain, particles of bone damaging the membrane.**

6. Why was Ziauddin irritated with all the people gathering at the hospital.

    A. **He felt the people were just waiting for Malala to die when they had done nothing to protect her.**

7. Malala's condition got worse. Explain.

    A. **Her brain was swelling and she was starting to deteriorate, her consciousness fading, and she was vomiting blood.**

8. What did her operation entail?

    A. **Doctors removed eight to ten centimeters of bone from Malala's skull, placed the bone under the left of her stomach (to be used later), performed a tracheotomy to help keep her airway clear, removed blood clots and the bullet from her shoulder.**

9. What did the two British doctors who were accidentally in Pakistan at the time discover about Malala's care?

    A. **There was no running water to wash their hands. Malala's blood pressure had not been taken for two hours, and her carbon dioxide levels were too low. Although she was "salvageable", her chance recovery was being compromised by the aftercare.**

10. What did Rehman Malik bring for Malala?

    A. **He brought her a passport.**

CHAPTER 22

Journey into the Unknown

1. By Thursday after she had been shot on Tuesday, Ziauddin was convinced that Malala would die. Explain.

    A. **Malala had been placed an induced coma, vital signs were deteriorating, face and body was swollen, and kidneys and lungs were failing. She had developed DIC (disseminated intravascular coagulation), she wasn't producing urine anymore, and her lactate levels had risen.**

2. What changes helped Malala survive?

    A.
    - **Dr. Fiona and two nurses stayed on in Peshawar to help Malala.**
    - **Malala was airlifted to an army hospital in Rawalpindi which had the best intensive care in Pakistan.**
    - **The nurses stayed with Malala, swapping antibiotics and blood lines.**

3. Why was helping Malala a critical decision for Dr. Fiona?

    A. **Dr. Fiona was a Westerner and if anything happened to Malala, it would have been blamed on the white woman.**

4. How was security handled while Malala was hospitalized?

   A.
   - **Hospital was on lockdown.**
   - **A battalion of soldiers were guarding the hospitals and snipers were on the roof.**
   - **Doctors had to wear uniforms.**
   - **Patients could only be visited by close relatives.**
   - **All mobile phones were confiscated.**

5. Not all reactions to the shooting were positive. Explain.

   A. Dr. Raheela Qazi from the religious Jamaat-e-Islami party called Malala an American stooge.

6. Why did Malala need to be moved again?

   A. It was likey Malala would need extensive rehabilitation and Pakistan didn't have any facilities for this.

7. How and where did Malala go?

   A. The ruling family of the United Arab Emirates offered a private jet, which had its own on-board hospital and could take Malala to Dr. Javid's hospital, Queen Elizabeth Hospital in Birmingham, England.

8. Why did Malala travel alone without her family?

   A. Malala's mother and brothers had no passports or documentation. Ziauddin was ordered to leave them behind and accompany Malala to England. But anything could happened if the family stayed behind, so Ziauddin stayed with the family and Dr. Fiona accompanied Malala.

PART FIVE
A Second Life

CHAPTER 23

"The Girl Shot in the Head, Birmingham"

1. What was the only thing Malala knew when she came around?

    A. Allah had blessed her with a new life.

2. Malala's recovery was a slow process. Explain.

    A.
    - **She woke up unable to speak.**
    - **Things seemed blurry. My eyes watered.**
    - **When she tried to write, the words came out wrong.**
    - **She suffered from severe headaches.**
    - **The left side of her face wasn't working properly.**
    - **Her mind was confused.**
    - **She forgot some English words.**

3. Besides recovering from her injuries, how did Malala feel when she woke up?

    A. Malala felt fear and bewilderment when she awoke.

4. What issues was Malala concerned with when she tried to communicate?

    A. She asked where was her father and who would pay for this treatment.

5. When did Malala first show excitement while recovering?

> **A.** She showed excitement when told they her they would be calling her parents.

6. What did Major General Ghulam Qamar mean when he said, "We are very happy <u>our</u> daughter has survived"?

> **A.** Malala was now seen as the daughter of the nation?

7. Why was Ziauddin so angry?

> **A.** He was angry when he found out twenty-two Taliban had been in town for at least two months and the army did nothing about it.

8. What evidence shows that Malala was curious about how she looked?

> **A.** She asked for a mirror.

9. Why can't people believe that a Muslim could attack me?

> **A.** Malala's mother would say, ". . .people call themselves Muslims, but their actions are not Islamic."

10. What did Malala's desperate mother threaten to do if arrangements could not be made for the family to leave?

> **A.** She threatened to go on a hunger strike.

11. How did Dr. Javid know that Malala's memory was fine?

> **A.** Malala could rattled off her mother's eleven digit mobile phone number.

12. What did Malala want from her parents when she learned they would be arriving in two days?

> **A.** Malala wanted her school bag with her books inside so she would be ready for her exams.

13. How did Malala pass the time in the hospital waiting for her parents to come?

A. **Dr. Fiona and the nurses played games with Malala. They brought her DVDs to watch movies.**

14.   Why wasn't Malala eating?

A. **She was worried the food was not halal. Halal food is food that which adheres to Islamic law, as defined in the Koran.**

15.   Who was the other Fiona?

A. **She was in charge of the hospital press office and began giving daily news briefings on Malala's condition.**

16.   Of all the gifts coming Malala's way, what were her favorites?

A. **Bilawal and Bakhtawar, children of Benazir Bhutto, sent Malala two shawls that had belonged to their mother.**

17.   What was the global meaning of "I am Malala"?

A. **This was a petition launched by Gordon Brown of the UN demanding no child be denied a school by 2015.**

CHAPTER 24

"They Have Snatched Her Smile"

1. How long had Malala and her family been separated?

   A. The sixteen days, four hospitals, thousands of miles separated Malala from her family.

2. Why did Ziauddin say, ". . .—they(Taliban) have snatched her smile"?

   A. The facial nerve in Malala's face was damaged.

3. Explain the simile, "It was like a reverse mirror."

   A. Every time Malala would laugh or try to smile, her mother's face would darken.

4. Who was Malala's attacker?

   A. The attacker, Ataullah Khan, had fled.

5. Who had unfairly been arrested?

   A. The bus driver, Usman Bhai Jan, was in custody to identify people.

6. More operations were to come. Explain.

    A.
    - **Dr. Richard Irving repaired her facial nerve.**
    - **Dr. Anwen White performed a titanium cranioplasty.**
    - **Dr. Irving put a cochlear implant to help with Malala's hearing.**

7. How could Malala identify with Dorothy from the The Wonderful Wizard of Oz?

    A. **Even Dorothy, who was trying to get home to Kansas, was helping people along the way.**

8. Where was Malala's first outing?

    A. **Hospital staff accompanied Malala to the Birmingham Botanical Gardens.**

9. What were the reasons Malala was allowed to meet with Pakistan's president, Asif Zardari?

    A.
    - **President Zardari was head of state.**
    - **The government was paying all of Malala's hospital bills.**
    - **They also rented an apartment for the family in Birmingham**

10. Why was meeting with President Zardari like a James Bond movie?

    A. **Malala was disguised in a hooded purple parka, taken down the staff entrance, then driven to the hospital offices.**

11. Why was the high commissioner told to give Ziauddin a post as education attache?

A. With this post, Ziauddin would not need to seek asylum to stay in the UK.

12. "...men and women chatting and mixing in a way that would be **unthinkable** in Swat.

13. Why did Malala laugh at the warning not be out late on Broad Street on the weekend?

   A. **The UK was not used to Taliban beheadings in Swat. That was dangerous!**

14. Who does Malala thank for her recovery?

   A. **She thanks God because she feels she was spared for a reason.**

EPILOGUE

One Child, One Teacher, One Book, One Pen. . .

1.   Why was the rented family home called a sub-jail?

     A.   The house is big and roomy but there are no neighbors visiting and rooftops to play on.

2.   How was the family home in the UK different from Swat?

     A.   My mother never turned anyone down if they were hungry and there were always visitors in Swat. In the UK, there was wasted food and an empty house.

3.   Describe in a short response how Malala's world has changed.

     A.   Accept any reasonable answer supported with evidence from the text.

4.   Respond to the following statement made by Malala's speech to the UN. "One child, one teacher, one book and one pen can change the world."

     A.   Accept any reasonable, thoughtful answer.

5.   Why does Malala still campaign for the right of education for all? Use evidence from the text?

     A.   Accept any reasonable answer with evidence.

6. In and essay, respond to the following statement at the end of the book. "I am Malala. My world has changed but I have not". Organize your essay and support your main ideas with details from the book.

WRITING WORKSHOP

THE ARGUMENT ESSAY

OVERVIEW	IMPORTANT ELEMENTS	TOPIC SELECTION
In preparing our students for college it is important to know that the argument essay may be one of the most common writing assignment they may encounter.	**Perform effective and thorough research** before committing to a topic to ensure enough credible resources for support. **Effective thesis statement** is important in any essay but especially important for the argument essay because the writer needs to identify the argument and why the argument is important. This cannot be confusing to the reader. **Necessary background information on the topic** supplies the needed details to support the thesis statement Because the argument essay involves multiple reasons and evidence to support overall thesis statement the writer should **focus on organization and transitions.** **Incorporate logos, pathos, and ethos** throughout the essay. Although logos (logic) should be the primary focus, pathos (emotion) can also be used for the argument essay. Ethos (credibility) is addressed by addressing counter arguments and using credible sources	**Current, debatable, researchable, and manageable** topics are best to use for the argument essay because they can be argued logically. A **current** topic is one that has not been over-debated and is still being decided. Avoid topics such as abortion, the death penalty, the legalization of marijuana. A **debatable** topic is controversial with differing viewpoints. Writing about domestic violence is not debatable since no one would disagree with this thesis. But debating whether common punishments for domestic violence are effective and a deterrent. A **researchable topic** can be supported with a variety of credible and current sources. A **manageable topic** is one that has been narrowed enough to meet the page requirement of the essay. Begin with a basic broad subject and then narrow it down to a subtopic.

CAUSE EFFECT ESSAY

OVERVIEW	TIPS
These essays are not to be about both causes and effects, but a focus on either cause or effect	**Introduction**—let your audience know what you are going write about. **Keep a narrow topical focus** and don't try to answer all causes or effects. Three or four is a good number to concentrate on. **Support all causes or effects with supporting details.** **Decide on the order in which to present information.** **Conclusion**—restate thesis or generalize your essay

COMPARE CONTRAST ESSAY

OVERVIEW	TIPS
These essays are huge in academic writing. They will follow a specific question and are fairly easy to complete. It is important to remember the structure and keep it consistent.	**Introduction**—like a five-paragraph essay, use a quotation, anecdote, generalization and then lead into the thesis statement. **Topic 1**—cover only the first topic of the comparison and contrast. Do not mention topic 2 in the first part. **Topic 2**—cover the second of the two topics. Do not discuss topic 1 here. **Topics 1 & 2 together**—Now analyze both topics together in one or multiple paragraphs. **Conclusions**—should be a generalization of the thesis as in introduction. Reaffirm your thesis. You complete knowledge of the subject should be apparent.

THE EVALUATION ESSAY

OVERVIEW	IMPORTANT ELEMENTS	TOPIC SELECTION
The purpose of an evaluation essay is to demonstrate the overall quality (or lack thereof) of a particular product, business, place, service, or program. While opinions are interjected naturally in this essay, if done properly the evaluation should seem reasoned and unbiased.	An overall **thesis** should be offered. Having clear **criteria** (ideal for the product/place/service/etc.) is what keeps an evaluation from feeling less like an opinion. The **judgment** is the establishment of whether or not the criterion is met. In other words, the judgment is what actually is. The **evidence** is the details offered to support the judgment Each body paragraph of an evaluation should **focus on one specific criterion,** which should be fully explained, followed by the judgment and a variety of evidence offered as support. Consequently all evaluations should contain several **different** criteria, judgments, and evidence	Focus on **specific business, service, product, or policy.** Write about a topic that you **have knowledge about** to make it easier to establish the appropriate criteria, judgments, and evidence.

THE INVESTIGATIVE ESSAY

OVERVIEW	IMPORTANT ELEMENTS	TOPIC SELECTION
Although similar to an argumentative essay, an investigative essay is often a precursor to an argument. The investigative essay allows for opinions and personal experiences, a difference from the argument essay.	In order to demonstrate a thorough knowledge of the subject, the writer **researches, researches, researches.** Writer must expertly interpret **research** and **articulate the various viewpoints** of the issue. The best investigative essays begin with a **legitimate question** to research, one that the writer is exploring.	**Current, debatable, researchable, and manageable** topics are best to use for the argument essay because they can be argued logically. A **current** topic is one that has not been over-debated and is still being decided. Avoid topics such as abortion, the death penalty, the legalization of marijuana. A **debatable** topic is controversial with differing viewpoints. Writing about domestic violence is not debatable since no one would disagree with this thesis. But debating whether common punishments for domestic violence are effective and a deterrent. A **researchable topic** can be supported with a variety of credible and current sources. A **manageable topic** is one that has been narrowed enough to meet the page requirement of the essay. Begin with a basic broad subject and then narrow it down to a subtopic.

PERSONAL ESSAY

OVERVIEW	TIPS
Often incorporating a variety of writing styles, the personal essay asks the writer to write about an important person, event, or time period in his/her life. The goal is to narrate this event in a way that uses both narrative and descriptive writing, which are two of the main models in writing.	**Focus on detail**—show, not tell using strong verbs, not overusing adjectives. **Use sensory detail**—bring the reader farther by using a variety of senses: sound, smell, touch, taste, in addition to sight. **Connect the event/person/place to a larger idea**—don't lose focus on the main idea: how the event changed you. It's the importance of the event that counts. **Be careful with verb tense**—when in doubt, stick with **past** tense for the actual event and **present** tense to discuss the change.

RESPONDING TO AN ESSAY

OVERVIEW	APPROACHES
Often following a literature summary, the writer responds to the piece subjectively using well -supported opinions and personal experiences. The thesis is the overall opinion of the essay you are responding to. Always be specific and always have support.	Agree or disagree with **the author's main point or thesis.** Agree or disagree with **the extent to which the thesis is made.** Agree or disagree with **specific points that are made that relate to the thesis.** Agree or disagree with **specific evidence that is offered in support of the thesis** Agree or disagree with **the relevancy of the overall topic.**

SUMMARIZING

OVERVIEW	TIPS
Although the shortest piece of writing in a high school course, it is not easy. A good summary accurately describes the main point and important details of the piece. In order to be accurate and concise the writer must be thoroughly familiar with the original work. If too long, a summary may be paraphrasing the original work, bit if too short, important details may be left out. Think one quarter to one third of the total length of the original article.	Read and **reread** essay as many times as necessary to gain a full understanding of it. No **first person statements** allowed. Opinions are not needed here. **Always name the author and article title** in the introductory paragraph, usually in the first or second sentence. From then on refer to author by **last name.** **Always use present tense** to discuss the essay and facts from the essay. Use **direct quotes or paraphrase** examples to support your claims. When talking about an essay or article, a**lways capitalize the title and place it in quotation marks.** Do not use italics.

USEFUL RESOURCES

Texts on Related Topics

Read *A Call to Action* by Jimmy Carter, which discusses global prospects for women's rights.

Related Websites

The Office of the UN Special Envoy for Global Education, go to http://educationenvoy.org/

The Malala Fund, go to http://malalafund.org/

The George Washington University, Global Women's Institute, developing *I Am Malala* curriculum (due out in Fall 2014). Go to http://gwtoday.gwu.edu/global-women's-institute-develop-'i-am-malala'- curriculum

The PBS site for a short video featuring Malala and questions for discussion: http://www.pbs.org/newshour/extra/daily_videos/malala-now-i-am-living-a- second-life/

C-SPAN2 features an interview with Malala Yousafzai, which was broadcasted in November 2013: https://archive.org/details/CSPAN2_20131102_173000_Book_Discussion_ on_I_Am_Malala

Keen University organized a panel discussion and their promotional website offers numerous news articles about Malala, a link to her diary, and other resources: http://sgei.kean.edu/i-am-malala

Malala's speech before the UN in July 2013 can be found at this site: http://www.youtube.com/watch?v=k_sIP08PZ6I

CPSIA information can be obtained
at www.ICGtesting.com
Printed in the USA
BVHW04s1638130818
524342BV00007B/234/P